HOUDINI

THE ULTIMATE
SPELLBINDER

HOUDINI

THE ULTIMATE
SPELLBINDER

BY TOM LALICKI

OPEN ROAD

INTEGRATED MEDIA

NEW YORK

All images are from the Variety Stage section of the McManus-Young Collection, Library of Congress.

These photos are part of the American Memory Collection of the Library of Congress: http://memory.loc.gov/

Copyright © 2000 by Tom Lalicki

Cover design by Stephanie Bart-Horvath

ISBN 978-1-4976-4477-9

This edition published in 2014 by Open Road Integrated Media, Inc.
345 Hudson Street
New York, NY 10014
www.openroadmedia.com

Houdini is surrounded by illustrations of the mysterious, magical, death-defying feats that made him legendary.

For Barbara

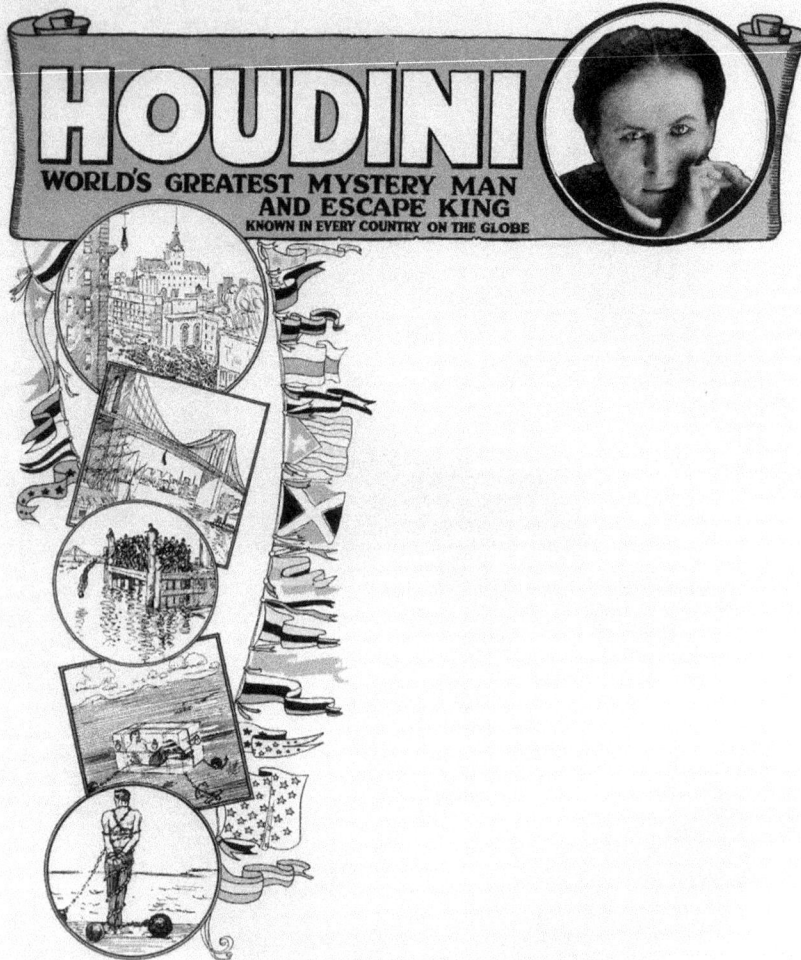

HOUDINI

**WORLD'S GREATEST MYSTERY MAN
AND ESCAPE KING**
KNOWN IN EVERY COUNTRY ON THE GLOBE

*One of the many letterheads Houdini
designed for his correspondence.*

The Greatest Novelty Mystery Act in the World!

In 1876, when Mayer Samuel Weiss sailed to seek his fortune in the New World, his hopes for the future must have been mingled with sadness and regret.

Trained as a lawyer, he could not practice law in his native city of Budapest because he was a Jew. He became a biblical scholar and a rabbi but could not find a congregation in Hungary. To make a life for his wife and five sons, Rabbi Weiss came to the United States alone. It took him two years to find a position.

Most Americans were Christians in 1876. The massive immigration of Eastern European Jews (and southern European Christians) started in the 1880s. Between 1880 and 1925, over 25 million people came to the United States —"The Golden Land"—to escape poverty and persecution. Not all the immigrants intended to stay. Called Birds of Passage, many intended to make their fortunes and go home rich. Over one third of all those immigrants did return to Europe, but almost none of them had become rich. They went back because making a life in America was just too hard for them.

In 1878, the Weiss family was reunited. The rabbi's wife, Cecilia, who was twelve years younger than Mayer, brought their four sons: Nathan, William, Ehrich, and Theodore. Herman, Weiss's oldest son from a previous marriage, came with them. Herman's mother, Mayer's first wife, had died years earlier. Two more children would be born in the United States: Leopold and Gladys.

Rabbi Weiss shepherded a small congregation in Appleton, Wisconsin, that worshiped in a room borrowed from a local club. Appleton was a beautiful, prosperous town. Its farmers grew wheat and its loggers cut trees to make paper. Appleton had a college, public parks, open, air concerts, and a welcoming attitude. The synagogue's members were German immigrants. Many of them had been encouraged to settle in Appleton after the Civil War, when Wisconsin and other Midwestern states had sent recruiters to Germany.

Congregation members flourished there, but Rabbi Weiss did not. He and his wife could not adapt to the "get-ahead" and "fit-in" mindset of nineteenth century America. They never learned English, the language his congregation members wanted their children to speak, so the congregation

An undated photograph of Houdini's father, Rabbi Mayer Samuel Weiss. He was a quiet, scholarly man who never adapted to life in the United States.

let him go. In search of another job, Rabbi Weiss moved his family to Milwaukee.

The rabbi's fifth son, Ehrich, the future Houdini, was a doer from his earliest days. Born on March 24, 1874 in Budapest, an old-world city, he was brimming with new-world energy. By the age of eight he helped support the family by working at street trades: shining shoes, selling newspapers, and running errands. His family desperately needed the money because Rabbi Weiss never found a steady job again. In Milwaukee, they moved five times because they couldn't pay the rent. A Jewish charity helped them out with food and coal.

In the 1880s, most children born in America went to school for seven years. Immigrant children got even less education. Ehrich was no exception, but he learned to read and write and loved to do both all his life.

He also loved to perform. At age nine, he debuted in a backyard circus, which had a five-cent admission, as "Ehrich, the Prince of Air." Decked out in red tights his mother had sewn, he did contortions—twisting body movements and trapeze walking.

Being the intelligent, ambitious son of an educated father reduced to poverty was painful for Ehrich, so painful that he ran away in 1886 to make the family's fortune. He was twelve. His mother, Cecilia, kept a postcard all her life that Ehrich had sent from the road. It said: "I am going to Galvaston, Texas [sic] and will be back home in about a year. My best regards to all.... Your truant son, Ehrich Weiss."

But he boarded the wrong train and ended up in Kansas City, Missouri. From there he worked his way back to Wisconsin by doing odd jobs. He was adopted for several months by the Flitcrofts of Delavan, Wisconsin, and finally made his way back home.

Impressed by his young son's pluck, Rabbi Weiss took Ehrich with him to New York on a job hunt in 1887. New York was the best place in the country for a German-speaking rabbi—nearly 80 percent of New Yorkers were either foreign-born or the children of immigrants.

They moved into a tenement on East Seventy-fifth Street in Manhattan. Ehrich's father taught German and Hebrew and occasionally performed religious ceremonies, but he could not support his large family. "We lived there, I mean starved there, several years," Houdini later remembered. As an adult Houdini never dwelled, though, on the economic hardships of his youth. He downplayed the family's poverty, writing, "The less said on the subject the better."

As a fabric-cutter in a necktie factory, the teenaged Ehrich shared the misery of the sweatshops. Suits, blouses, gloves— every kind of clothing was made in dark, overcrowded tenements. Sanitary conditions were so bad that tuberculosis was called "the tailor's disease." Immigrants worked ten to fourteen hours a day, six, even seven, days a week. The pay, about three dollars per week, was too little to support a family, so the entire family worked.

Children as young as eight, called "lively elves," were prized by sweatshop owners. Children had nimble fingers for sewing and were easily disciplined. If they didn't take their work seriously enough, the penalties were severe. Looking out a window without permission cost a day's pay.

Most young people were exhausted, if not ruined, by the system. Not Ehrich Weiss. He found time and energy to box in the 115-pound class, to swim in the East River, and to run distance races for the Pastime Athletic Club. And he loved to pick through the used-book bins on Fourth Avenue and haggle over the prices of books he wanted to read. He often read late into the night. He did not seem to think his life was hard.

Nobody knows when Ehrich (nicknamed "Ehrie") became seriously interested in magic. He may have given a show in 1890 on a trip to Milwaukee, or he may have debuted in New York that same year. But it's certain that by 1892 "The Brothers Houdini: The Modern Monarchs of Mystery" were professional showmen. And eighteen-year-old Ehrie Weiss was, then and forever, Harry Houdini.

Ehrich had read and loved the memoirs of Jean Eugene Robert- Houdin, known as the father of modern magic.

Ehrich Weiss, soon to be Houdini, poses as a confident champion at the age of sixteen. He won the medals for boxing, cross-country running, and swimming in his spare time, after putting in a full day at the factory.

Robert-Houdin had abandoned the age-old wizard's costume—flowing robe and pointed hat—for black evening dress. His conjuring devices were placed on a raised, undraped platform that made trapdoors and help from assistants seem impossible. Ehrich idolized him and wrote, "From the moment I began to study the art, he became my guide and hero. His memoirs gave to the profession a dignity worth attaining at the cost of earnest, life-long endeavor." In tribute, Ehrich adopted and adapted his hero's name. (Later in life, he autographed books: "Houdini. That's Enough." One name said it all.)

In the fall of 1892, Rabbi Weiss died of cancer. He left behind a wife who spoke no English and two children under sixteen. Before dying, the rabbi asked his promising young son to swear that he would always care for his mother. Houdini kept that promise.

Show business is an uncertain way to make a living at the best of times, and those were not the best of times. The Panic of 1893 started with falling stock prices and quickly staggered the nation. By year's end, five hundred banks and nearly sixteen thousand businesses had failed. Unemployment rose to 20 percent in an era before federal unemployment insurance and welfare. With no money, the unemployed became homeless and stood on breadlines for food. In Chicago, thousands of people lived through the winter sleeping in the hallways of City Hall. "Ruin and disaster run riot over the land" was a British observer's description.

The economy improved in 1895, but a second recession set in the next year. The country did not fully recover until 1901. Ehrich Weiss could have returned to cutting necktie fabric—he had a standing offer from his old employer. Instead, Houdini pressed on in show business.

The "Brothers Houdini" were Ehrich and a friend, Jack Hyman, who quickly left, seeking greener pastures. The next Houdini brother was Ehrich's real brother, Theo, who was in the act until Houdini met his life partner in 1894.

Like many times, places, and events in Houdini's life,

it's uncertain how Houdini first met Wilhelmina Beatrice "Bess" Rahner. But it is certain that he fell madly in love with her, completely and forever. They were married less than a month after meeting and honeymooned at Coney Island.

Houdini's mother took instantly to Bess and never objected to her son's marrying a Catholic. Cecilia welcomed the newlyweds into the already crowded Weiss family apartment. Bess's mother was a widowed German immigrant and devout Roman Catholic. She objected passionately to the marriage and refused to talk to her daughter for more than ten years.

"The Houdinis" were not only husband and wife, but also magician and assistant. Houdini was about five feet, five inches tall with thick, wiry black hair, intense blue eyes, and a large head. Fiercely strong and muscular from years of conditioning, he seemed large compared to the five-foot-tall, ninety-pound, brown-haired Bess. Onstage, he wore

Poised and confident, Bess and Harry in their first picture as a married couple. It's also their first professional picture, but their last as "The Rahners: America's Greatest Comedy Team." They were not very good comedians.

Metamorphosis was the Houdinis' first successful escape.
The illustrations fanned out around Harry and Bess
show the audience what to expect at the theater.

secondhand evening clothes and she wore heavy woolen tights topped with puffy blouses.

While Houdini had been perfecting card tricks and other common conjuring tricks for several years, the focal point of the Houdinis' act was Metamorphosis, a substitution illusion he had bought from another magician.

Buying tricks was not unusuaL Most magicians' acts are based on the work of retiring or hard-up magicians who sell their secrets and their apparatus. Houdini paid twenty-five dollars—a small fortune— for Metamorphosis: a steamer trunk, a large three-sided cabinet that closed in front with a curtain, and the secret that made it entertaining.

A "committee" of audience volunteers would come onstage and inspect all the props. Houdini then stepped inside a large flannel bag inside the steamer trunk. The committee taped the bag shut and sealed it with hot wax. Houdini sat in the trunk, which was padlocked and circled with heavy ropes. Then Bess spoke.

"I shall clap my hands three times, and at the third and last time I ask you to watch closely for...the...effect." She swung the curtain shut in front of the trunk and disappeared. Instantaneously, the curtain opened to reveal Houdini himself. Furiously the committee unknotted the ropes, unlocked the padlocks, opened the trunk, pulled up and unsealed the still taped bag to find...Bess.

The King of Handcuffs

Vaudeville, the variety stage show, was the premier family entertainment then. Singers, comedians, dancers, impersonators, comedy singers, comedy dancers, and magicians filled out affordable three-hour shows for growing city audiences.

After the Civil War (1861-65), America's population was growing and becoming more urban. Before the war, about six million Americans lived in cities; by 1900 the number was over thirty million. The number of cities with populations of more than fifty thousand people mushroomed, too: from sixteen before the Civil War to seventy-eight by 1900.

The growth of cities was fueled by the Industrial Revolution. Factories that turned out such modern conveniences as ready-to-wear clothes, canned food, and bicycles needed laborers. While most of the immigrant workers filling the cities had little money or leisure time, factory managers, office workers, and professionals did.

But cities in the 1890s offered few recreational activities. Without cars or public transportation, people were limited to their neighborhoods. Without television, radio, or CDs, families had to entertain themselves. Even telephones were too expensive for most people. Nickelodeons showed primitive movies that were brief, not very exciting, and actually cost a dime. That same dime could buy real entertainment-vaudeville.

Promoters built lavish theaters, decorated with huge chandeliers, pillars, and murals that gave audiences comfortable places to relax and see first-rate shows. There were several tiers of vaudeville theaters. The best acts played the Keith-Albee Circuit of theaters on the East Coast and the Orpheum Circuit in the West. But in 1894, Mr. and Mrs. Houdini were far from prime-time players.

Ranked below vaudeville were the Dime Museums, an outgrowth of P. T. Barnum's Museums. There magicians, jugglers, and puppeteers were jumbled together with curiosity, or curio,"acts like sword swallowers, fire eaters, midgets, giants, and fat ladies. Performers did from twelve to twenty shows a day for very low wages. Even recent immigrants could understand and afford these shows.

The bottom rung of urban entertainment was the beer hall, where noisy and not very interested patrons enjoyed corny one-act plays and sentimental songs. Small, town folk needed entertainment, too, and that was offered by traveling burlesque, or girlie, shows, circuses, and medicine shows.

Between 1894 and 1899, the Houdinis learned the craft of showmanship by performing in all these arenas, struggling to make ends meet the whole time. To get bookings, they did a song-and-dance act and appeared in very bad plays.

Houdini and Bess (front row right) as members of the Welsh Brothers Circus. In addition to their magic act, they did a Punch and Judy Show, a song and dance number, mind reading, and Houdini played "Projea, the Wild Man.

Houdini performed as "Projea, the Wild Man" in an animal cage and did a mind-reading act and onstage séances.

The séances were electrifying. Houdini came into a small town with a show and, incredibly, knew personal things about total strangers sitting in the audience. It was all sham, but very convincing. Ahead of the show, Houdini would sneak into town and do some very sharp detective work. He would loiter in barber shops for gossip, read old newspaper files, and pretend to be a Bible salesman to get into homes and get personal information about families. Armed with a smattering of facts and aided by paid local help who could identify audience members, Houdini could accurately retell the past and predict the future.

Popular as the act was, Houdini abandoned it almost immediately. He wrote in his diary that the séances produced a "Bad Effect!" Houdini wanted to mystify his audiences with skill, not scare or cheat them.

Regardless of how little Houdini earned, he honored the promise to care for his mother. When he and Bess had bookings, half their weekly salary was always sent to Cecilia. When they didn't, the Houdinis shared her Manhattan apartment while Houdini worked on schemes to improve the act.

A less determined, less confident man would have given up entirely and taken a job. The closest Houdini came to that was opening a correspondence school for magicians in his mother's apartment. He offered all his secrets for sale. Luckily, nobody thought the tricks worth buying.

The problem with Houdini's act was that he hadn't yet discovered the real Houdini. He performed as "The King of Cards," "The King of Billiard Balls," even as "The Paper Tearing King," without much success. Audiences loved the Metamorphosis escape but did not love Houdini's magic tricks. He worked constantly to develop new ones. He watched and studied hundreds of other performers to learn showmanship. He improved his grammar and stage speech. Most importantly, he invented brilliant ways to promote the act. But none of his efforts opened the door to stardom.

This publicity shot shocked viewers in the 1890s. A naked man in chains escaping from a jail cell was very daring and very exciting.

In 1895, Houdini let audience members handcuff him (with their own handcuffs) as part of Metamorphosis. He escaped. Then he let the police of Gloucester, Massachusetts, lock him in their handcuffs. And he escaped. In Woonsocket, Rhode Island, police and newspaper reporters shackled Houdini with six sets of handcuffs and locked him in a room. He escaped in eighteen seconds.

It was terrific advertising in those relatively small towns, but it went no farther. In the days before national news magazines, radio, and television, Houdini's escape from police handcuffs in Woonsocket was purely local news.

At first, the handcuff routine was not a success onstage, either. Bess Houdini remembered: "All our acts went well with one exception. That was the handcuffs....Our small-town American spectators were utterly cold to it. The majority of them apparently assumed that Houdini was using prepared [trick] cuffs."

Another trademark trick that Houdini developed during this time was the straitjacket escape—a stunning feat of strength and agility nobody else could match.

Professional strongmen and bodybuilders appeared on the vaudeville stage, but they had nothing on Houdini. Houdini's powerful body was the foundation of his success. He developed it by swimming in the East River and running in Central Park. He became ironlike, with massively muscled forearms and thighs. He never drank alcohol or smoked because strength and endurance were his most precious assets.

During a Canadian tour, Houdini visited a mental hospital and watched violent patients writhing on, the floor to free themselves from straitjackets. Determined to escape from a straitjacket himself, Houdini borrowed one and had Bess wrap him in it. She restrained him in the jacket seven times before he devised a technique for escaping. It left him swollen, bruised, and bloody.

Onstage, the cabinet curtain was drawn closed as the straitjacketed Houdini twisted, turned, and rolled on the floor until, free, he opened the curtain holding the empty canvas coat. This stunt didn't catch on right away, either. Audiences thought it was a cheat. Nobody could escape from a real straitjacket, so they assumed Houdini's was rigged. The trick was a flop.

Houdini didn't give up on either the handcuff or the straitjacket escape. Houdini never gave up on a good idea. If audiences didn't like an escape he liked, he tried to improve

HOW DOES HOUDINI DO WHAT HOUDINI DOES?

HOUDINI---The name conjures up Jails, Prisons, Handcuffs, Bolts, and Bars, for he is the creator of that branch of work. A daring man, skillful, careful entertainer, and never having met with defeat, he is open to accept any challenge during his engagement at the Orpheum Theatre the coming week, that will interest the general public. When not accepting a challenge, during his regulation performance, he will introduce his original invention, "The Chinese Water Torture Cell." Houdini is the only legitimate jail-breaker in the world and was proclaimed by Theodore Roosevelt "The Most Stupendous Mystifier I Have Ever Seen." Let us hope he will receive some interesting challenges, and that our local carpenters, locksmiths and other craftsmen will construct something from which Houdini cannot extricate himself.

The Genius of Escape
HOUDINI
Who Will Startle and Amaze

Orpheum
MAIN 4161

Orpheum Circuit Vaudeville
ONE WEEK ONLY

Starting Saturday Matinee

MAY 5th

SAME POPULAR PRICES—NEVER CHANGE
Daily Matinees, 15c to 50c   Every Night, 15c to $1.00

Handcuffs, jails, straitjackets, packing crates, tire chains –
Houdini could escape from anything or anywhere. People loved
to ask: "Just how does Houdini do what Houdini does?"

the presentation. He had the patience and determination to keep going back over a problem until it was solved.

While playing a Minneapolis beer hall in the spring of 1899, lightning struck Houdini's floundering career. Martin Beck, who ran the entire Orpheum vaudeville circuit, liked Metamorphosis and the handcuff escape. He told Houdini to drop the card, billiard ball, and paper-tearing tricks from the act. Beck wanted Houdini to do a twenty-minute turn in the top vaudeville theaters for sixty dollars a week—more than he had ever earned before. Houdini wrote that the offer "changed my whole Life's journey."

Like a jewel under a bright light, Houdini responded to attention by revealing brilliant new facets. Now he played only two shows a day, not twelve. He stayed in cities for a week or more, not one night. This gave him the time and the platform to experiment with his act and impress his audience.

He constantly improved Metamorphosis. He sometimes

borrowed a suit jacket from the audience, which he would
put on before going into the trunk. After the switch, Bess
would emerge wearing the borrowed jacket. Sometimes he
took people into the trunk who escaped with him.

Responding to an accusation that he used keys to open
handcuffs, Houdini went to a San Francisco police station
on July 13, 1899. He was stripped naked and examined by
a police surgeon who certified that he was hiding nothing.
His mouth was taped shut, his wrists and ankles were
shackled in ten sets of police handcuffs. For good measure,
the ankle cuffs were attached to the handcuffs with an
eleventh pair before he was locked into an interrogation
room. Five minutes later Houdini walked out, still "——"
(the way most polite newspapers spelled the word *naked*
then), carrying all the cuffs in his hands.

In April 1900, again nude, he took just three minutes
to escape from a doubly locked jail cell in Kansas City. He
repeated these escapes wherever the police allowed. Each

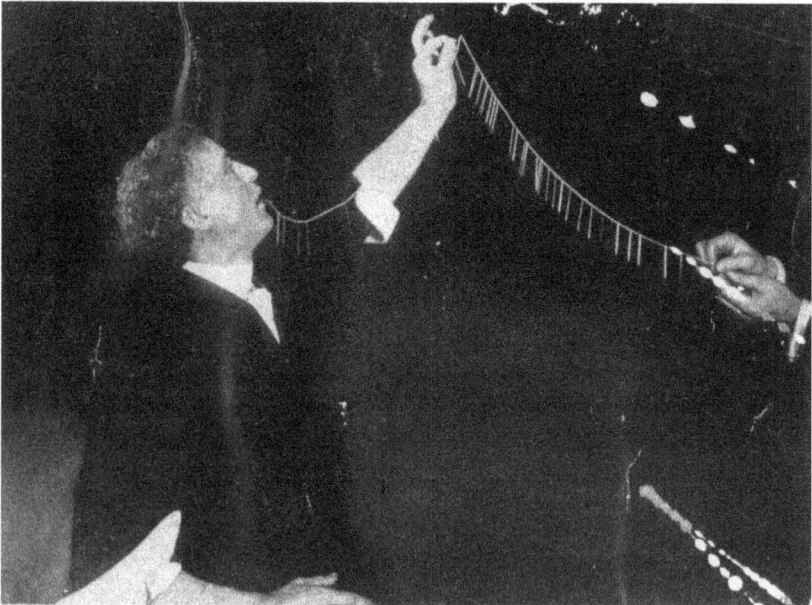

*Houdini swallowing needles in 1915. For more than
twenty-five years, audiences were mystified and examining
physicians were baffled by this trick introduced in 1899.*

police force added new obstacles, almost desperate not to be embarrassed by this upstart magician. But they always were. And as Houdini knew, the stories written about him by big-city newspapers were the most valuable and cheapest advertising available.

The public commotion he caused generated massive interest in his stage act and sold tickets. His $60 salary rapidly increased to $250 a week—half the total yearly income of an average American worker.

Houdini also introduced another new trick that, like Metamorphosis, would continue to thrill audiences for his entire career. To perform the East Indian Needles, Houdini called an audience committee onstage to look into his nose and throat. Nothing hidden there. He swallowed a handful of sewing needles, loudly chewing on them and washing them down with water. Next, he swallowed a ball of sewing thread. Then he put his hand into his mouth and slowly drew out the thread with the needles threaded on it.

Although profoundly successful, Houdini needed more. The Houdini legend was started and continuously reinforced by a tireless engine churning out mountains of promotion. The engine was Houdini's mind. A 1900 flyer he sent to theater managers announced:

WHERE THE POSSIBILITY CEASES, THE IMPOSSIBILITY COMMENCES!... HARRY HOUDINI, "KING OF HANDCUFFS," **DEFIES** DUPLICATION, EXPLANATION, IMITATION OR CONTRADICTION.

The Sensation of Europe

In May 1900, barely a year after being catapulted into stardom, Houdini was dissatisfied. He needed new audiences to dazzle and mystify. Booked for American appearances beginning in August, he postponed them and sailed to Great Britain instead. He had no work lined up and no manager in London, but he had unlimited confidence.

It seemed as though conquering Europe had always been in the cards for Houdini. In 1895, a Houdini poster had falsely claimed that he had headlined in London, Cambridge, and Oxford—cities he'd never even seen. In the United States, a country still unsure of its taste and place in the world, anything popular in Europe seemed more valuable, even escape artists.

After a tryout, Houdini was booked for two weeks in July 1900 at the Alhambra Theater in London, a top hall that held more than four thousand people. Houdini sold it out. His two weeks turned into two months and a return for the Christmas season. A typical review called him "probably the most mysterious and wonderful entertainer the world has ever seen." To keep the standard handcuffs/ Metamorphosis act fresh, Houdini continued to polish his performance skills.

He sported elegant evening clothes: a frock coat (knee-length tails), a stiff white collar, and a white bow tie. He introduced the "ghost cabinet": a short, three-sided, draped enclosure. Manacled behind the back, he stood inside the cabinet with his face and upper body visible to the audience — a unique spectacle. Twisting and turning to free himself,

The Alhambra Theatre was named for the palace of the Moorish kings of Granada, Spain. There were five hundred variety theaters in the London area, and Houdini started his 1900 tour at the best.

pain clear on his face, Houdini made the audience part of the struggle. That was new and daring.

The next stop was Germany, officially the Second German Empire, ruled by Kaiser Wilhelm II. Germany in 1900 was an authoritarian country where order and conformity were enforced by a huge, powerful, even feared, state police force. Before being allowed to perform, entertainers had to submit their entire show for police approval. People were put in jail for misleading the public, which was what Houdini did for a living. Houdini called it mystification, not fraud, but the police wanted proof.

*Houdini's 1900 escape at Berlin's police headquarters
was so vividly remembered by Germans that he used the
incident to advertise a performance eight years later.*

At a command performance in Berlin's police headquarters, three hundred policemen watched as Houdini was stripped naked and examined. His arms were locked behind his back with police thumbscrews, finger locks, handcuffs, and leg irons. His mouth was taped shut. Then his iron-bound body was wrapped in a blanket and put on an examination table.

It took Houdini just six minutes to escape. The police grudgingly gave him this endorsement: "At this time, we are unable to explain the way in which the locks are opened and remain undamaged." Even though the police were not very enthusiastic, the German people certainly were. Overflow crowds bought standing room tickets and packed the aisles of every German theater Houdini played.

Commanding salaries higher than he could get at home, Houdini settled in for what became a four-and-a-half-year stay. Again and again, he played to sellout crowds in England, Scotland, and Germany, with trips to Russia, Holland, and France sandwiched in. He became a perennial favorite by establishing a routine: "I lost no time in stirring up local interest in every town I played. The first thing was to break out of jail."

Europe had no Wild West filled with shoot-outs and jail breaks. That may be why Houdini's symbolic defiance of authority was more exciting in cities such as Edinburgh and Amsterdam than it was in the United States. Escaping nude from a fortress-like prison used by Oliver Cromwell or jail cells that once held well-known murderers became "town-talk at once," according to Houdini.

He was "The World's One and Only Handcuff King." Like a champion boxer, Houdini was determined to keep the title. Dozens of handcuff release acts sprang up to compete with Houdini's. They used gaffed, or prepared, handcuffs, and their claims of superiority over Houdini infuriated him.

The cover of a four-page publicity brochure that included pictures of Houdini in action, thirty-seven reviews of his act and the addresses of his British and American agents.

TREMENDOUS SUCCESS
OF
HOUDINI

"Absolutely a Miracle."—
Supt. MELVILLE,
SCOTLAND YARD
Detective Headquarters.

"Certainly an Astounding Mystery."—
INSPECTOR ROBERTS,
Bow Street
Police Headquarters.

"A very smart Show, and certainly requires a bit of doing."—
SERGT. BUSH,
Chief Gaoler.
Bow Street.

The King of Handcuffs.
THE SENSATION OF LONDON.

Houdini actually missed performances in order to infiltrate imitators' shows and defy them to beat him.

None ever did. Houdini's ability to open any lock was, simply, magical.

There have always been people who claimed to explain how Houdini did the handcuff escapes: He carried hidden keys, Bess passed keys to him when she kissed him onstage, he had lock picks or tiny pieces of wire hidden on his naked body. There are hundreds of explanations, but none is true beyond doubt.

One of his most famous handcuff releases took place in 1904. The *London Illustrated Mirror* challenged Houdini to escape from a set of cuffs it had made specially for the purpose of defeating him.

The Bramah lock had been created for locking up government secrets. A challenge offering three thousand dollars to anyone who could pick that type of lock had stood unclaimed for more than fifty years until an American locksmith succeeded. With the Bramah lock in front of him on a table, the locksmith had taken forty-four hours to pick it. The *London Illustrated Mirror* Challenge handcuffs were built from two Bramah locks nested one inside the other.

Houdini had the double-locked cuffs closed behind his back during a packed matinee performance. Completely hidden behind a curtain, he struggled for a half hour, then emerged to thunderous applause. But he was still cuffed.

During the performance he asked for a pillow to kneel on and a glass of water. Then he asked for the cuffs to be opened so that he could remove his coat. The newspaper representative refused: If Houdini saw how the key opened the cuffs, it would give him an unfair advantage.

Fair enough. In front of the curtain, Houdini fished a pocket knife from his jacket, opened it with his teeth and slashed until he had shredded his jacket and let it fall away.

Near the one-hour mark, he walked behind the curtain again. In the audience, some whispered among themselves while others yelled encouragement. Almost no one had left the theater; he had everyone's total attention.

Harry Handcuff Houdini.

Houdini holds a copy of The Illustrated Mirror handcuffs — probably the most complicated set of cuffs ever made. Seventy-five newspapers wrote stories about his incredible escape from them.

Finally, Houdini bounded out and thrust the open handcuffs skyward. Another challenge defied. The audience exploded; it roared approval.

Houdini had become a spellbinder. Some politicians were called spellbinders because their speeches held audiences spellbound. Houdini was unique—he kept audiences enthralled as he silently grimaced and twitched behind a curtain.

But how did he do it? Was it all an elaborate fake? Did he have the key?

Did he have the keys hidden to open all the locks the German police had used in 1900? Hardly! Two of the cornerstones of Houdini's success were his pride and his work ethic. An almost desperate fear of failing in public made him work fanatically to succeed.

Houdini practiced opening locks incessantly. He even apprenticed himself to locksmiths. He collected hundreds of handcuffs and leg irons to work on. He never wanted to be surprised on stage by having a lock type put on that he didn't know. Still, when that inevitably happened, he would succeed in opening it.

How did he actually open a specific lock on a given day? The best answer is the punch line to an old vaudeville joke that asked, "How do I get to Carnegie Hall?" The answer is: "Practice, practice, practice."

Practice prepared Houdini for inhuman challenges. A physical fitness expert in Blackburn, England, tied and locked him up so tightly that witnesses thought Houdini's blood flow was cut off and he might die. After nearly two hours of struggling, he was free, but one reporter wrote that Houdini "looked as though some tiger had clawed him." In Germany, a straitjacket was applied so viciously that it prompted Houdini to say, "The pain, torture, agony and misery of that struggle will forever live in my mind." Sometimes he was so tightly cuffed that his wrists were too sore to do a handcuff escape again for a week.

Houdini's biggest accomplishment in Europe was putting a new twist on the trunk escape and making it even more interesting. In the Packing Case Escape (1902), Houdini escaped from a box supplied by a local manufacturer rather than his own prop trunk. When he was nailed and roped into the box by the workmen who made it, what trickery could there be?

For two years, dozens of such boxes were brought onstage to confound Houdini, and he escaped them all. In the process, the supplier got advertising, Houdini got newspaper space, and theater managers saw houses filled by employees of the box companies and their families.

The Handcuff King's path wasn't always smooth, but it

was unswerving. He refused to allow his reputation to be tarnished, because he depended on it for his livelihood.

Accused of being a fraud by a policeman in Cologne, Germany, Houdini sued the policeman for slander. Houdini won the case by performing an escape in the courtroom. The policeman appealed twice to higher courts and lost both times. Judges could not deny that Houdini lived up to his own advertising, and Houdini reveled in it. "It does seem strange," he wrote, "that the people over here fear the Police so much, in fact the police are all Mighty, and I am the first man who has ever dared them, that is my success."

He printed and gave away thousands of promotional posters announcing his victory over the German state. He made dozens of other posters to keep people thinking about Houdini. He even gave away press-on decals so that his face would be on his fans' front windows.

One poster commemorated his only trip to czarist Russia in 1903. Houdini was successful there but had no desire to return.

He had been forced to travel on Bess's passport. Jews were forbidden entrance to Russia, but since Bess was Roman Catholic the couple was allowed in. The border search was so frightening that Houdini sent his diaries and notes back to Germany rather than let the secret police examine them.

Still, Houdini fearlessly challenged the secret police to lock him in a "Siberia Wagon"—a prison cell on wheels used to carry prisoners thousands of miles to remote prisons.

The escape was done privately and the police refused Houdini the promotional seal of approval he had been promised. Nobody knows exactly what happened, but a large, illustrated poster he gave away in Western Europe enhanced the growing Houdini legend. It pictured him "stripped stark naked" before being locked in the prison cell on wheels. The poster's copy boasted that "in 28 minutes Houdini made his escape to the unspeakable astonishment of the Russian police." After that escape Houdini performed for large audiences in several Russian cities and dined as a guest of the royal family. Still, his diary noted that leaving Russia was like "escaping from a mild prison."

We know what Houdini thought about practically everything from his diaries. He started keeping them in the mid-1890s with a notebook given away by a Detroit newspaper, and he filled dozens more. He seemed to use whatever fell to hand—from tiny pocket notebooks to huge financial ledgers. He wrote about performances, other performers, and everyone he met. He recorded ideas and plans for new escapes. He avoided politics and religion, but the Russian trip prompted this comment on anti-Semitism: "It may exist in America, but never that I have known. I never was ashamed to acknowledge that I was a Jew, and never will be, but it is awful what I hear from people that are Jew Haters."

Not outwardly religious, Houdini practiced one Jewish ritual faithfully. Every year on the anniversary of his father's death, Houdini sought out a synagogue and said Kaddish, the prayer for the dead.

The diaries point to one sadness of his life—the lack of children. "We have been married for 10 years and all we have is a 'dog.' ... Perhaps in 1905 we may rest long enough to raise one of them things called children ourselves." The Houdinis never had a child but always had pets that they loved profoundly. The loss of their first dog, Charlie, saddened Bess and Houdini for months. Charlie had traveled everywhere with them, magically hidden from border guards as they moved between countries.

The World's Greatest Escape Artist

Between 1900 and 1905, Houdini returned to the United States only twice; he did not perform there either time. In Europe, he said, "the sun shines for me every day." He was making at least a thousand dollars a week. He was being modest when he wrote, "Pretty good for Dime Museum Harry."

By this time, Bess no longer had equal billing or an equal share in the act. She continued to perform Metamorphosis for decades, but the substitution trick was no longer the core of Houdini's act. Strenuous, dangerous escapes were the attraction; only Houdini could do them. Bess settled in to the role of road manager. She dealt with Houdini's assistants, travel arrangements, wardrobe, and all the other detail work necessary to keep the act moving.

Being on the move month after month made Houdini long to see his mother. During a 1904 vacation, he bought a four-story brownstone in the Harlem neighborhood of New York City, then a fashionable area for affluent German immigrants. Cecilia and Houdini's sister, Gladys, moved into the brownstone, at 278 West 113th Street, as Houdini and Bess sailed back for another season in Europe.

Houdini was Europe's brightest star, but he knew that he would be forgotten in America unless he came back and toured with brilliant new escapes. Most vaudeville specialty performers kept a headliner status for two or three years, then drifted lower down the bill—audiences became bored by familiar, repetitive acts.

*"I have loved two women in my time," Houdini wrote. They
were his mother, Cecilia Weiss, and his wife, Bess.*

Houdini feared sinking into obscurity, and possibly
poverty. He had grown up watching that happen to his
father. Fortunately, he was bursting with ideas and energy
and always found a new trick when he needed one.

The new "homequarters" at 278 doubled as home and
laboratory. In an oversized, sunken bathtub, Houdini spent
hours in ice baths to acclimate himself to the cold. He
practiced holding his breath until he could last well over
three minutes without breathing. He sketched new escapes.
He kept both his fingers and toes limber by practicing card
tricks. And he filled the second-floor library with books.

In Europe, Houdini started collecting books, playbills,
posters—anything related to the history of magic. Eventually
he owned more than five thousand books on magic and
substantial collections on related subjects like Spiritualism
and superstition. On tour, he would bring along a writing
desk, a portable typewriter, and about one hundred pounds
of books—he was an avid reader and letter writer.

At the turn of the twentieth century people were

fascinated by crime and detection. Sherlock Holmes had taken the world by storm, and the memoirs of policemen and professional criminals were very popular. In 1906, Houdini became a public-spirited author. *The Right Way to Do Wrong* told readers how to avoid being victimized by pickpockets, confidence tricksters, and other petty thieves.

The world's greatest escape artist (NOTHING ON EARTH CAN HOLD HOUDINI A PRISONER, said one poster) had no sympathy for criminals. Some offered to buy

Bess stands by calmly as her husband prepares to dive, chained and handcuffed, into Boston Harbor. Mrs. Houdini was as certain of her husband's abilities as he was.

Houdini's secrets, but they would have been useless even if Houdini had sold them. Performing his escapes demanded a package of skill, knowledge, trickery, and, most of all, fearlessness—a combination only Houdini himself possessed.

Houdini proved his fearlessness as he crisscrossed the United States from 1905 to 1908 with dangerous new escapes. Hundreds of thou- sands of spectators in different cities saw, for example, the Manacled Bridge Jump. Wearing a skintight swimsuit, his arms chained and hand, cuffed behind his back, Houdini jumped from bridges into rivers and freed himself underwater. The stunt was very dangerous; any small mistake would have meant death. But Houdini was not reckless. Using his swimming skills, the ability to hold his breath, his knowledge of locks, and his steely nerve, he made the escape look easy. Imitators were seriously injured, even killed, trying to copy him.

No matter what impossible feat Houdini attempted, he attracted imitators. He completely dropped handcuff escapes because there were so many copycats. Houdini said, "If you throw a stone in the air it will fall down and hit some one who has a handcuff key in his pocket."

He slept five hours a night at best. "I have tried through many a sleepless night," he said, "to invent schemes to make an audience appreciate some worthy effort of mine."

In 1908, Houdini triumphed again. In a booming showman's voice, with every word carefully enunciated, Houdini said: "Ladies and Gentlemen, my latest invention— the Milk Can. I will be placed in this can and it will be filled with water. A committee from the audience will lock the padlocks and place the keys down in front of the footlights. I will attempt to escape. Should anything happen, and should I fail to appear within a certain time, my assistants will open the curtains, rush in, smash the Milk Can and do everything possible to save my life .... Music, Maestro, please!"

Then he crammed himself into the can. Water was poured in, covering his head. The can was locked and the curtain drawn around the can. Houdini's trusted assistant, Franz Kukol, raised his fire ax and stared anxiously at the curtain.

To spectators, it seemed like an eternity was passing and that Houdini must be drowning.

After three minutes, the curtain flew open. A soaking-wet and breathless Houdini stood on a dry floor beside the still-locked can. The audience, breathless and stunned, broke into thunderous applause.

"Failure means a drowning death" was how the Milk Can Escape was advertised. Totally submerged in water, with his body doubled over and hands chained, Houdini had no margin for error.

Houdini continued to thrill audiences with this death-defier for years. It didn't matter whether or not exposers explained the trick or copycats did cheap imitations, what Houdini did with the Milk Can Escape was exciting and dangerous.

Houdini was convinced that continued success depended upon hazardous escapes. The easiest way to attract a crowd," he wrote, "is to let it be known that at a given time and a given place some one is going to attempt something that in the event of failure will mean sudden death."

Knowing that "sudden death" was an all-too-real possibility, he brought Cecilia to Rochester, New York, in 1908 to watch a Manacled Bridge Jump just in case it was his last performance. Before another jump, he handed Kukol an envelope with a quickly scrawled will leaving everything to Bess.

Probably the only thing Houdini really worried about was not doing enough for the women in his life. Bess and he spent five months on the road and seven months off, sharing 278 with his mother. Houdini often took Cecilia on shopping excursions and walks. He read to her while she cooked and baked. He was a model son but regretted being away from her so often. It was partially guilt that had brought the Houdinis back to the United States in 1905.

Houdini and Bess, meanwhile, were as affectionate as

As thousands look on, Houdini dives into Boston's Charles River. There were so many spectators in boats that space in the water had to be cleared before he could jump.

newlyweds all their lives. Working upstairs in the library, Houdini loved nothing better than "hearing Mrs. Houdini call up, 'Young man, your lunch is ready.'" Bess kept the hundreds of love notes he wrote his life long. And he had hundreds of endearing names for her: "Beatrice Beautiful Houdini," "Winsome Wilhelmina," "Darling-Darling Darling." In his scrapbooks, Houdini kept all the notes she had written to him, even messages as mundane as "Chicken in the ice-box—pie on the pantry shelf."

Houdini's second book, *The Unmasking of Robert-Houdin*, was published in 1908. He intended the book to be a definitive history of magic, but it became an unfortunate expose of his childhood hero. Research had convinced Houdini that Robert-Houdin had not invented many of the illusions he had claimed as his own. Houdini's brutal criticism and his calling Robert-Houdin the "Prince of Pilferers" infuriated other magicians. Whether or not Robert-Houdin had been the genius he had claimed to be, the man had modernized and dignified the practice of magic. On the other hand, Houdini's praise for his father in the book's dedication may seem extravagant. Houdini wrote: "The book is affectionately dedicated to the memory of my father, Rev. M. S. Weiss, Ph.D, LL.D, who instilled in me love of study and patience in research."

It's uncertain what Houdini learned from his father, but it's clear that he remembered him fondly. Houdini's theater dressing table always had a photograph of his father on it, and he listened to recordings he had made of his father's poetry. When a reporter asked the name of his favorite author, Houdini proudly said, "My dad."

Always trying to improve the act, Houdini reworked his Packing Case Escape and called it the Open Challenge. He challenged well-known companies to defeat him with their products, and dozens tried. Houdini escaped from the world's largest paper envelope without tearing it, from the world's largest football, from a locked U.S. Postal Service mailbag, and from a commercial boiler that had been welded shut.

It was great fun for audiences just to see what sort of
odd prison would be created to foil Houdini. The Weed
Tire Chain Grip Company used snow chains, automobile
wheels, and plenty of padlocks to bind and weigh him down.
Carried into the cabinet, it took Houdini nineteen minutes
of clanging and thrashing to break free. It was stunning
theater.

Every American city he played was dazzled by a Manacled
Bridge Jump, at least one Open Challenge, and nightly Milk
Can Escapes. As if by magic, a Houdini who could mystify
had gone to Europe and returned as a Houdini who could
electrify. This power was deeply rooted in dedication and
hard work, but the results excited even Houdini: "Sometimes
I think that these stunts hold far greater thrills for me than
they have even for the spectators."

*To attract ticket buyers, Houdini always had a theater-
lobby display that highlighted his accomplishments.*

The Prince of Air

Today, we would say that Houdini was on the cutting edge. Before record players were made to be portable, he took them on the road. He wired 278 with intercoms and listening devices. Houdini liked knowing how things worked, and he very much liked being first.

When Houdini and Bess returned to Europe in 1909, "Ehrich, the Prince of Air" became Houdini the airman. He suffered from violent seasickness, and he couldn't drive a car. But just one look at an airplane convinced him that there was "magic in flight."

For five thousand dollars, Houdini bought a Voisin plane, hired a mechanic named Brassac, and had his name painted in giant letters on the side panels. Every morning for two months, after performing two shows the night before, Houdini would be driven to his plane, where he would sit and wait for good weather.

Good weather and good luck were crucial for pilots in those first days of flight. Engines were small and planes were made of light, fragile materials to help lift them off the ground. An unexpected strong wind could crumple a plane's wings like paper.

The first time he went up over Hamburg, Germany, Houdini flew less than a hundred feet before crashing. The plane was rebuilt, and his next flight lasted a little more than a minute. Never disheartened by failure, Houdini framed a goal for his flying adventures: He would set a record by becoming the first man to fly over the continent of Australia.

An Australian theater manager tempted Houdini to make the long trip by offering him full salary during the weeks of

In 1910, a Melbourne newspaper published this photographic collage to celebrate the first successful flight over the Australian continent.

sailing there and back. He would be seasick the entire trip, but he couldn't resist the notion that "I receive full salary while onboard the steamer...twelve weeks for doing nothing."

In Australia, for the first time in his career, Houdini's attention was not focused on his act. Outside Melbourne, he and Brassac erected a forty-foot-square tent where they worked for weeks, reassembling and testing the Voisin biplane.

Houdini was completely exhausted. He had lost twenty pounds during the ocean voyage and arrived during the 100-plus-degree days of the Australian summer. After doing his nightly shows, he often drove to the makeshift hangar and spent the night there to be ready to work or wait, or maybe even fly, at dawn.

Finally, on March 18, 1910, Houdini made three flights. Witnessed by reporters, Houdini stayed aloft for over three minutes at an altitude of 100 feet. He told the *Sydney Herald*, 'As soon as I was aloft all the tension and strain left me....All

*Houdini flies. Long before the Goodyear Blimp was created,
Houdini combined the magic of flight with advertising.*

my muscles relaxed, and I sat back feeling a sense of ease, freedom and exhilaration."

Recognition and awards followed, and Houdini reveled in "the glory of having been the first successful Australian aviator." Characteristically, he joked that it was a "pity I can't carry enough petrol [fuel] to fly home with my good wife." Charles Lindbergh would not make the first transoceanic flight until seventeen years later.

Houdini never flew again after leaving Australia. Flying had rewarded him with a few minutes of exhilaration and tons of free publicity. It had cost him a small fortune in money and time. It was a hobby he cheerfully dropped.

That was very unusual. Most of Houdini's interests were lifelong and deeply felt. From 1900 on, he tracked down retired performers to learn about the history of magic. He bought the belongings of down-and-out magicians to give them the "dignity" a magician should have. He paid for many funerals, gave food and rent money to widows, and tended to graves. If a magician's grave was ignored, he would restore it and pay to have flowers delivered regularly. In Australia, he bought a permanent grave site for William Davenport, a world-famous American illusionist who had died there on tour.

William Davenport's partner, his brother Ira, was still alive. Houdini visited him in 1910. Houdini felt that the "Davenports stand forth in [the] nineteenth century history of magic as its most dramatic figures." But not everybody called the Davenports magicians. Believers in Spiritualism thought they were mediums—people who communicated with the spirits of the dead.

Modem Spiritualism began in 1848 when it was discovered that two adolescent girls in upstate New York, the Fox sisters, seemed to have received messages from beyond the grave. Spirits answered the questions of the living by making rapping noises. The Fox sisters became celebrities. Managed by P. T. Barnum, they performed all over the country. Even though one sister later confessed that the messages were phony—produced by cracking their toe joints—the craze was unstoppable.

The Davenport Brothers became famous with a more sophisticated act. They were rope-tied and locked inside a "spirit cabinet" that contained musical instruments. They were obviously unable to move because of the restraints, but as soon as the cabinet was locked, the instruments began to play and fly around the stage in the dark. When the cabinet was opened, the brothers were still tied and the musical instruments were still inside. While the Davenports never claimed to have help from the dead, thousands of believers thought otherwise.

Houdini, who had read minds and conducted séances years earlier, got the truth from Ira Davenport: "Strange how people imagine things in the dark! Why, the musical instruments never left our hands, yet many spectators would have taken an oath that they heard them flying over their heads." Ira also showed

After the Davenport Brothers and their assistant (center) were locked in the cabinet and the theater was darkened, instruments appeared to fly about and play themselves. Audiences thought the brothers were in contact with spirits, but the brothers styled themselves "performers."

him the secret "Davenport rope ties" that let the brothers untie and retie themselves almost instantaneously.

By the 1870s, Spiritualist mediums were submitting to "challenges" to prove that they were really in touch with the supernatural world. Some were examined naked to prove they were not hiding tools. Some were bound by handcuffs and ropes to prove that they were not manipulating objects in the dark. Spiritualists claimed that they could not escape from their fetters and that things flew about because spirits had made them fly. In fact, Spiritualists surreptitiously used mechanical escape trickery to convince audiences that they possessed genuine supernatural powers.

Houdini knew better. He turned Spiritualist tricks upside

Houdini spent more than three years perfecting the Chinese Water Torture Cell escape before its debut in 1912. Dangerous and demanding, the "Upside Down Trick" thrilled audiences for nearly fifteen years.

down. He wasn't a medium and didn't contact the dead—
he made escaping the entertainment. More times than he
wanted to, Houdini made this point: "Everything I do is
accomplished by material means, humanly possible, no
matter how baffling it is to the layman."

Preparing his most baffling, most frightening, most
thrilling stage illusion was the next item on Houdini's
agenda. In 1910, Houdini hired James Collins, a British
carpenter. Collins helped him build an illusion that Houdini
had planned for three years. Costing over ten thousand
dollars, the trick was kept a secret until September 12, 1912,
when, at the Circus Busch in Berlin, Houdini introduced
"the greatest sensational mystery ever attempted in this or
any age"—the Chinese Water-Torture Cell.

Center-stage was a narrow glass box with wooden
corners that looked like a telephone booth. While Houdini
was offstage changing into a swimsuit, music played and the
tank, or cell, was filled with water. Houdini returned and
lay on the stage while the cell's top, which had holes for his
feet, was snapped around his ankles.

A winch pulled Houdini into the air directly above the
water-torture cell. Slowly he was lowered, upside down, into
the cell. Houdini was completely submerged in the glass cell
with his shoulders touching the glass, his hands probing, his
hair floating in the water.

The assistants slammed the lid's padlocks and drew the
curtain closed. Trick or not, it was clear to an audience that
this was scary business.

An assistant stood by with an ax, ready to smash the glass.
A giant stopwatch over the cell clicked away the seconds. An
orchestra played a song called "Asleep in the Deep." Then
suddenly, Houdini startled the crowd by bounding out from
behind the curtain, dripping wet and struggling for air. The
cell was still locked and filled with water; the floor around
it was dry.

Houdini had topped himself, and the competition, again.
"I believe," he said, "that it is the climax of all my studies
and labors .... Never will I be able to construct anything that

will be more dangerous or difficult for me to do." Within months, copycats were doing inferior imitations.

Houdini sued the imitators and won decrees to make them stop. It infuriated him that others profited from his ideas, but the public knew there was only one real Houdini.

Unfortunately, the real Houdini was beginning to feel his age—thirty-eight. He constantly threatened to retire. The act was hard on his body and he knew he couldn't continue it forever. Still, he electrified the country that same year with an outdoor escape *Scientific American* called "one of the most remarkable tricks ever performed."

This advertising copy describes his 1912 escape:

HOUDINI, SECURELY HANDCUFFED AND LEG IRONED, WILL BE PLACED IN A HEAVY PACKING CASE, WHICH WILL BE NAILED AND ROPED, THEN ENCIRCLED BY STEEL BANDS, FIRMLY NAILED. TWO HUNDRED POUNDS OF IRON WEIGHTS WILL THEN BE LASHED TO THIS BOX CONTAINING **HOUDINI**. THE BOX WILL THEN BE **THROWN INTO THE RIVER**. HOUDINI WILL UNDERTAKE TO RELEASE HIMSELF WHILST SUBMERGED UNDER WATER.

New York City police, standing on a tugboat filled with reporters, told Houdini he couldn't jump into New York Harbor. Well, if nothing on earth could hold Houdini a prisoner, nothing and nobody on water could stop his act before it started. Houdini had the tug steam out to Governor's Island. There, in waters controlled by the U.S. government, the box went overboard with Houdini inside.

Less than a minute later, Houdini's head bobbed out of the water.

Chains hauled up the wooden crate and it was still intact. The ropes and steel bands were secure; inside were the chains and locks Houdini had left behind. To the cheers of thousands on nearby boats, Houdini had once again miraculously, unbelievably, defied death.

This packing case, shut with nails, chains and steel bands, was lowered into New York Harbor with a manacled Houdini inside. A minute later, Houdini swam to the surface. When the crate was hauled up, it was still sealed tight.

The Grand Magical Revue

The death of his mother in July 1913 shattered Houdini. He had just arrived in Denmark when he found out, and he returned on the next ship. Contrary to Jewish practice, Houdini asked his brothers and sister not to bury Cecilia until he could see her one last time. She had asked him to buy woolen bedroom slippers for her, which he placed tenderly in her casket. Then Mrs. Weiss was buried near her husband and stepson in the plot Houdini had purchased for the family years earlier.

Houdini deeply loved his mother, but the travel demands of his career kept him away from her company much of the time.

A rare gathering of the Weiss brothers in 1911. From left to right: Leo, Theo (Hardeen), Ehrich, Bill, and Nat.

Houdini felt guilty because his career had kept him away so often. Unable to accept the natural death of his aged mother, he went into a shell of mourning. He locked up 278 because the memories there over-whelmed him. Houdini and Bess moved into his brother Theo's Brooklyn home so that Houdini could recover.

Theo had been in the act until Houdini married Bess. When Houdini took Europe by storm in 1900, he cabled Theo, saying, "Come over. The apples are Ripe!" He outfitted Theo with an act like his own, named him Hardeen, and helped him get bookings.

Hardeen succeeded as a magician, but he was always second-rate compared to his brother. Nobody was capable of equaling Houdini, but it must have hurt to be introduced as "the brother of the Great Houdini." Even as a guest in Hardeen's house, Houdini expected top billing. The brothers soon realized that they could not live under the same roof.

Not ready to move back into 278 and uncomfortable in his brother's home, Houdini went back to work. He returned to Europe to fulfill old contracts, but he was a saddened man. His stationery carried a black mourning wreath. He carried a book of all his mother's letters to him, typed to read more easily. Even the satisfaction he got from performing was

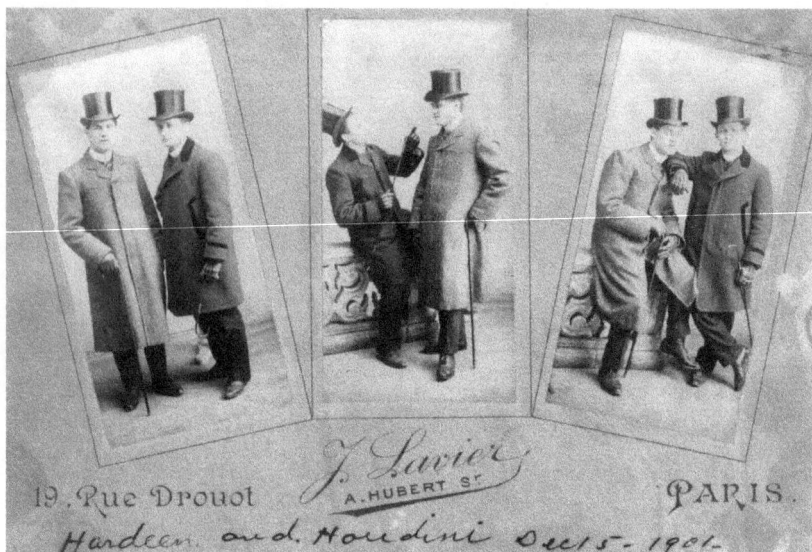

19. Rue Drouot   J. Lavier
                        A.HUBERT Sᵗ   PARIS.
        Hardeen and Houdini Dec 15 - 1901.

*Houdini with Brother Theo in Paris, 1901. Houdini
had equipped his brother's act, made his bookings
and even chosen his stage name: Hardeen.*

overshadowed by his loss: "Some times I feel alright, but
when a calm moment arrives I am as bad as ever."

Despite his sadness, Houdini forged ahead. Before returning
to New York in the summer of 1914, he realized a lifetime
dream. Staged at enormous expense, the *Grand Magical
Revue* was opened in England. It was an hour-long Houdini
show with no escapes. It featured magic—coins vanished, torn
cloth was mended, Lady Godiva rode a disappearing pony.

It was not successful. Audiences wanted Houdini
the escapologist, not Houdini the magician. After ten
performances, Houdini boarded a ship for New York and
left nearly all the magic props behind.

Even shipboard, before long-distance telephone service,
Houdini managed to make headlines in New York. Theodore
Roosevelt, the former President of the United States, was
treated to a unique Houdini presentation during the trip.

Entertainers routinely performed for passengers during
sea voyages, and Houdini relished the opportunity, if he
wasn't seasick, to do pure magic. On this trip he agreed to
a séance trick—slate-writing. The trick normally involved

holding two chalkboards together while someday asked the medium a question. When the slates were turned over, an answer to the question would have "magically appeared."

In the ship's lounge, Roosevelt was asked to write his question secretly, away from Houdini's sight. His question was: "Where was I last Christmas?" Houdini revealed a slate with a map of the southernmost tip of South America drawn on it. There was an arrow pointing to an area labeled THE RIVER OF DOUBT.

Astonishingly, that was where Roosevelt had spent his previous Christmas. How could Houdini have known that? Roosevelt asked if this was an example of genuine Spiritualism.

"It was hocus-pocus," Houdini replied.

Finding out that Roosevelt would be sailing on his ship, Houdini had convinced a newspaper friend to get him prepublication copies of magazine articles Roosevelt had written. Houdini learned all the facts he needed to prepare the map before sailing. Talking with Roosevelt, Houdini suggested the right question without the former president catching on.

Houdini was so proud to be photographed with President Theodore Roosevelt that he had an airbrush artist remove the other five people from the photograph. He gave away thousands of the version showing Houdini alone with Roosevelt.

Houdini handed Roosevelt a book, for support, while Roosevelt wrote his question. Inside the book's cover, Houdini had hidden carbon paper over blank writing paper. Taking the book back from Roosevelt, he slipped it open unseen and read the question he had hoped for. With a little more sleight of hand, Houdini was able to produce the correct slate. Very skillful hocus-pocus, indeed.

Ship-to-shore radio screamed "Houdini!" However, the Roosevelt "demonstration" shared front pages with rumors of a coming European war.

Months later, in August 1914, the Great War, also called World War I, swept across Europe. Thirty-two countries and 65 million soldiers fought—four years of relentless horror.

The very first battles saw cavalry charges and soldiers marching behind military bands. Those old techniques were quickly replaced by the tools of modern warfare: machine guns, barbed wire, long-range artillery, tanks, and poison gas.

The kings of Germany, Austria, and Russia were overthrown. The map of Europe was redrawn as Czechoslovakia, Yugoslavia, and Hungary were created. By November 11, 1918, at least 10 million soldiers were dead and another 20 million had been wounded.

In 1914, most Americans called it Europe's War. The United States declared itself neutral and most Americans tried to ignore it. Entertainers like Houdini helped them.

Houdini had brought a theatrical surprise back to New York called Walking Through a Brick Wall. In the act he did just that.

Twice a day masons built a high wall onstage, brick by brick. A large committee of audience members pulled a rug taut across the stage and then placed a muslin cloth over it. The committee members stood in two semicircles as the brick wall was wheeled in place between them.

Houdini stood on one side of the wall as a three-sided, six-foot screen was pushed against it, enclosing him. An identical screen was then placed against the wall's opposite side.

Houdini waved his hand above the screen and said, "Here I am. Now I'm gone." As his hand disappeared, the screen was pulled away, proving him right. The other screen was pulled aside immediately, revealing Houdini. He was standing on the other side of the wall as if he had walked through it.

At this stage in his career, Houdini was an absolute master of mystification and showmanship. He had learned to "walk down to the footlights, actually put one foot over the electric globes as if I were going to spring among the people, and then hurl my voice" to grab their attention. He made spectators think about the thrills and danger in store. After all, 90 percent of the time the audience was listening to Houdini or watching a drawn curtain!

He worked audiences, drawing them into the performance. And he could joke, too. Before doing a Packing Case Escape,

Houdini performs the Suspended Straitjacket Escape opposite the Treasury Department in Washington, DC.

he philosophically said, "If I succeed, it's a fine trick; if I don't, it's a good chest."

Houdini dropped the brick wall illusion quickly, because another magician claimed to have invented it, and Houdini did not do other people's illusions. He passed it on to brother Hardeen.

In 1915, Houdini first did the "outside stunt" that won him the most fame—the Suspended Straitjacket Escape. This release illustrates another reason for Houdini's success.

Traveling circuses did parades through every town they played— showing off their freaks and animals, letting their performers do previews. Before mass media like radio and TV existed, a circus parade was the most effective form of advertising for a show coming into town.

But Houdini made promotion into an event. Rather than making lots of noise and hoping to attract passersby, Houdini printed flyers, gave newspaper interviews, did everything in his power to attract a crowd to witness a spectacle.

Bridge jumps, underwater escapes, and Suspended Straitjacket Escapes weren't previews of anything. They were compelling theatrical performances done for free, performed before millions of people who would never see Houdini in a theater—but they would remember him all their lives.

Who could forget the drama of seeing a small man with graying hair painfully cinched up in a straitjacket, turned upside down, and pulled hundreds of feet into the air by his ankles? Swaying in the wind, Houdini began his fight to free himself. Twisting and turning, sometimes "standing" upright on the ropes, he struggled. It went on for minutes until he extended his arms, the jacket off and in his hands. Then he dropped it to the street below.

He had found a road where imitators feared to tread— just what he had always been looking for. "I want to be first," he told a reporter, "first in my profession.... I have tortured my body and risked my life only for that—to have one plank on the stage where the imitators cannot come, and one spot where they all fall back and cry 'Master!'"

Houdini's free performances weren't limited to potential

ticket-buyers. Nearly once a week, Houdini performed in retirement homes, orphanages, and children's hospitals. If you couldn't come to Houdini, he came to you. Applying his almost religious work ethic to charity, he devised a show just for the blind.

When the need arose, he gave to his country just as freely. After the United States declared war on Germany and the other Central Powers on April 6, 1917, Houdini immediately volunteered for the army. He was rejected. Houdini, one of the world's fittest men, was forty-three years old; the government wanted men aged thirty and under.

When Houdini was suspended upside down in a strait jacket, he always saw huge crowds below like this one.

Houdini works his magic for hospital patients. He did sleight-of-hand card and coin-tricks during visits to hospitals and nursing homes.

To support the war effort, all citizens were asked to make sacrifices. Government agents went door-to-door asking residents to observe a meatless day and a wheatless day every week. Heatless Mondays conserved coal for use by supply ships traveling to Europe. The war was paid for through Liberty Bonds, and posters encouraged citizens to "give until it hurts."

Houdini answered the call. Canceling profitable bookings, he sold Liberty Bonds and performed in dozens of troop camps. He put some money in soldiers' pockets, too: Money for Nothing was a coin trick in which Houdini made gold coins appear out of thin air. He materialized thousands of gold coins during these shows, and all of them went to soldiers in the audience.

Patriotism spurred Houdini to reveal his professional secrets for the sake of American servicemen. In a makeshift classroom, he showed soldiers how to escape from German-made handcuffs. He taught sailors techniques for surviving a shipwreck: breathing underwater, opening locked doors, and untangling ropes.

Beginning to feel his age, Houdini needed a way to

make his act less demanding. After debuting the outdoors straitjacket escape, he said, "I've about reached the limit.... Hereafter I intend to work entirely with my brain." Houdini knew from experience that "the audience never knows whether the stunt is hard or easy." He had dropped some escapes because they were tortuous for him but looked simple to audiences.

On New Year's Day, 1918, Houdini introduced his biggest, most eye-popping illusion—one that put no strain on him. In the Vanishing Elephant, he made Jenny (supposedly the daughter of P. T. Barnum's world-renowned Jumbo) vanish onstage. Even Houdini's magician colleagues thought it was a splendid trick. He paired the world's largest illusion with his most intimate trick—the East Indian Needles.

What could Houdini do next?

The Vanishing Elephant, Houdini's largest illusion. For nineteen weeks—the longest engagement of his career— Houdini made Jenny disappear.

The World-Famous Cinema Star

Movies had arrived and Houdini wanted in. Around 1900, most films were ten-minute curiosities. They were silent, barely moving pictures of exotic lands. They were shown in stores where patrons sat on folding chairs. By World War I, hour-long Westerns and adventure films played in real theaters. They were still silent, but every theater had a pianist or organist who played music that moved the story along. Some theaters had full orchestras. By 1920, forty million movie tickets were being sold every week.

For years, Houdini used film footage of his bridge jumps and flying exploits during his shows. But "motion picture palaces" bigger than vaudeville theaters were built. Movies were here to stay.

In 1916, Houdini opened a business called the Film Development Corporation in West Hoboken, New Jersey. The company did high-speed film processing and appeared to be a surefire moneymaker. Friends invested and brother Hardeen eventually managed the business full-time. But Houdini was not very smart about money. He spent fortunes as fast as he earned them and made poor investments. The Film Development Corporation never succeeded and actually lost a great deal of money.

In front of the camera, Houdini was an instant success. His first film, *The Master Mystery*, was a fifteen-episode serial. Cliff-hangers, as serials were called, were the perfect format for Houdini. As the plot unfolded bit by bit, the star was left each week facing certain death. Whether dangling

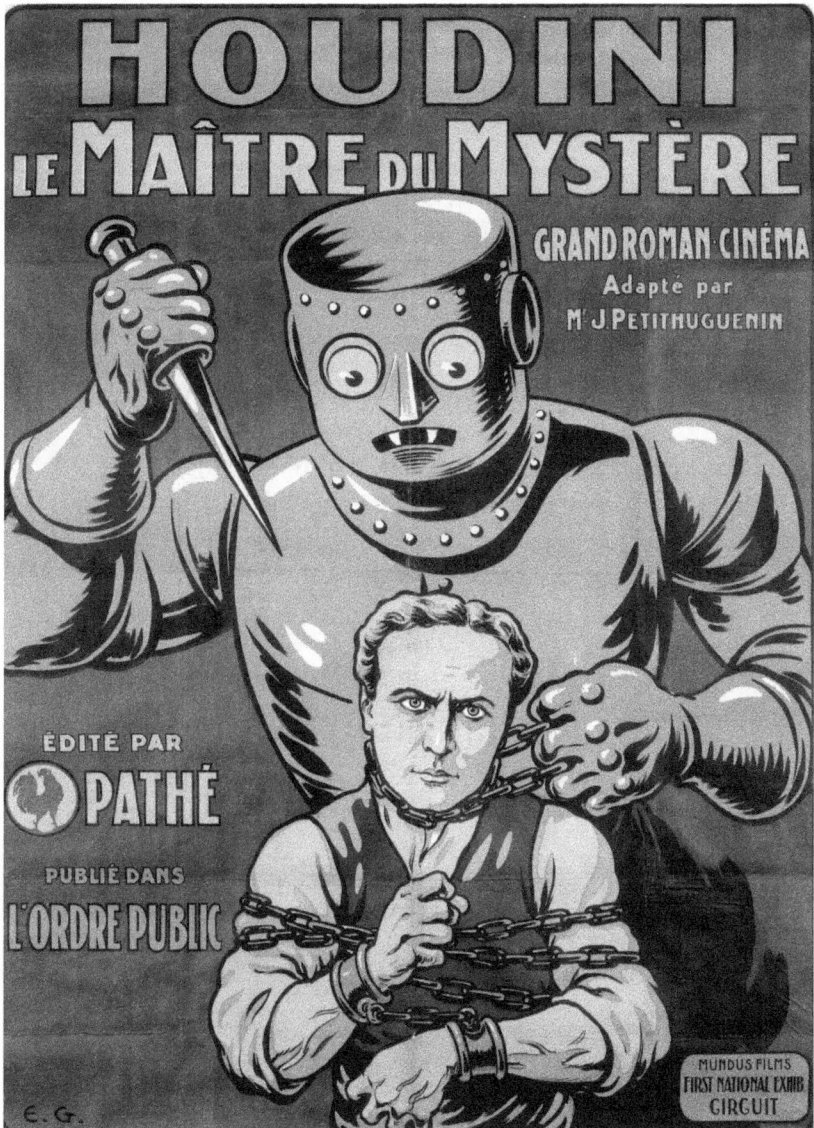

Houdini's first film, The Master Mystery, was a hit around the world.

over a cliff or about to be sawed in half, the hero or heroine left audiences wondering and waiting for a week to see how he or she would escape. In the next episode of Houdini's first film, "the Master of Escape" always succeeded and eventually defeated the villains and won the girl's undying love.

The Master Mystery debuted in 1919 and audiences around the world ate it up. Houdini shared in very large profits. In France, he was billed as "The Most Popular Man in the *Entire* World."

Next, he signed with an up-and-coming studio that became Paramount Pictures, and made *The Grim Game* (1919) and *Terror Island* (1920). Houdini was wildly enthusiastic about his films. After all, he was wildly enthusiastic about all his accomplishments. But he kept a sense of humor about his self-promotion. Writing to a friend about *The Grim Game*, he pronounced it "the Greatest Melodram[a] ever seen. (Am still as modest as usual.)"

Filled with daring exploits and hair' raising stunts, each succeeding Houdini film was less successful than the one before, and the studio dropped his contract. The films suffered from two serious problems.

First, Houdini himself quickly realized that "no illusion

Advertising proclaimed that "Houdini Pictures Corporation presents the wizard of all ages, Houdini, in the thriller of photoplay history The Man From Beyond who....lay frozen in a mass of ice for 100 years, only to be...brought back to life to live the most stunning story ever told."

is good in a film, and we simply resort to camera *trix* and the deed is did." He suffered more broken bones and torn muscles—even an accidental stabbing—making films than he did onstage, but audiences *knew* that movies were trickery.

Second, Houdini's acting ability was limited. Kenneth Silverman, a Houdini biographer familiar with these hard-to-find films, says, "His acting consists of three expressions: pucker-lipped flirtatiousness, open-eyed surprise, and brow-knitted distress."

Disregarding criticism, Houdini was certain that movie making was a "good trick," he just needed to figure out how to present himself. So he opened his own studio in the early 1920s—the Houdini Picture Corporation of New York—to control the process.

His last two pictures, *The Man From Beyond* (1922) and *Haldane of the Secret Service* (1923), were no better than earlier films, but these were costing him money. To guarantee full houses for *The Man From Beyond*, Houdini paid three traveling magic companies to tour with the film and perform between showings. His movie career and the film developing business were the biggest setbacks of his career.

But movies did give him something new that he treasured—free evenings to do research and write. In 1921, *Miracle Mongers and Their Methods* was published. Describing the ways that fire eaters, sword swallowers, poison defiers, and other "freak" acts performed their "miracles," it was a loving tribute to performers he had worked with. He wrote: "The Dime Museum is but a memory now, and in three generations it will, in all probability, be utterly forgotten." Houdini didn't want the players to be forgotten as well.

A Magician Among the Spirits

A new passion gripped Houdini in the 1920s. He had held the public's attention, entertaining people with handcuffs and packing cases and straitjackets for more than twenty years. Now he had a cause.

"I am waging war on the fraud mediums in this country," he wrote. He said that the fees mediums charged for pretending to contact the dead were "the dirtiest money earned on this earth." Phony Spiritualists caused "EXPLOITATION AND MISERY."

Popular belief in Spiritualism had come and gone after the popular noise-making feats of the Fox sisters. But World War 1 changed every, thing. Ten million died in combat. And in the fall of 1918, just before peace returned, an epidemic of influenza swept across the war-torn world. That flu, in a time before vaccines and antibiotics, killed another 20 million people.

By 1920 practically everybody in England had lost a close relative, and the belief in Spiritualism mushroomed there. Surveys reported that one in every three English men and women thought it was possible to communicate with the spirits of the dead.

Sir Arthur Conan Doyle, creator of Sherlock Holmes, emerged as a self-proclaimed prophet of this new religion. Calling Spiritualism "absolutely the most important development in the whole history of the human race," Doyle claimed to speak with his dead son regularly during séances. He believed that spirits could be photographed and could levitate tables and open doors—tricks Houdini knew any good magician could do without the help of spirits. No matter how often spirit manifestations proved to be false, Doyle found an excuse. His faith was unshakable, much like that of people who are sure they've traveled in alien spaceships.

In 1920, Houdini and Doyle became friends, but the relationship did not last. The two men ended up bickering about each other in the pages of *The New York Times* and other major newspapers.

Spiritualism stirred up very painful emotions in Houdini. He was certain that every medium he had ever seen was a fake, yet he longed to contact the spirit of Cecilia, his mother. He spent hours at his mother's graveside and often woke in the night speaking her name. "My mind has always been open and receptive and ready to believe," he said about séances. Any cost was worth the reward of reaching his dear mother: "I, too, would have parted gladly with a large share of my earthly possessions for the solace of one word from my loved departed." Even after hundreds of failures, he still hoped to find a genuine medium who could establish contact with his mother. But he showed no mercy for people who tricked the innocent public.

Houdini the Crusader took to the road to expose fraudulent mediums. He crisscrossed America in 1924, lecturing about the evils caused by crooked mediums. "I have watched this great wave of Spiritualism sweep the world in recent months," he wrote, "and realized ... that it has become a menace to health and sanity." He told how people committed suicide, even murdered their own children, to become reunited with lost loved ones. Mediums charged for each séance, and they often made spectacular amounts of money. It was quite common for voices from beyond the grave to encourage the living to give away everything they owned to the medium conducting the séance.

Houdini's *A Magician Among the Spirits*, published that year, told the long history of medium frauds and revealed the tricks these magicians-gone-bad used to fleece at least a two-dollar fee from vulnerable customers.

Scientific American magazine offered a $2,500 cash prize to any medium who could convince its committee of scientific experts, one of whom was Houdini, that he or she was genuine. A number of mediums competed for the prize, but their tricks were quickly exposed. Then an unexpected challenger stepped forward, one who would hold Houdini's, and the American public's, attention for more than a year.

Mina Crandon was the attractive, soft-spoken wife of a famous Boston surgeon. To protect her identity, she was called "Margery" in newspaper reports. By the time Houdini heard about Margery in June 1924, committee members had already attended over thirty séances at the Crandon home and were leaning toward awarding her the prize.

Houdini was angered that he had been excluded from

Psychic investigators O. D. Munn and J. Malcolm Bird, and Houdini with Mina Crandon outside her Boston home. Known to the public as Margery, Mina Crandon battled with Houdini to prove she was authentic. The conflict made headlines for months.

this case. He suspected immediately that J. Malcom Bird, a *Scientific American* editor and the committee's secretary, was too sympathetic toward Margery. Houdini demanded that more séances be held, and he rearranged his performance schedule to attend them.

After Houdini's first séance with Margery, he said, "I've got her. All fraud." But the committee wasn't convinced.

During the séance Margery contacted a "spirit-control" named Walter, her dead brother. Walter made furniture move

Houdini inside the wooden cabinet he made to test Margery's psychic abilities. He used the box during anti-Spiritualist lectures to prove that Margery's talents were physical, not psychic.

and rang a bell attached to a box in the middle of the room. Houdini was sure that Margery had freed herself in the dark to accomplish her tricks, but the committee wanted proof.

For later séances, Houdini and James Collins built a wooden cabinet for Margery. Locked in, with only her arms and head poking out of the box, the effects stopped. It seemed, by the fifth Houdini séance, that Margery had been proved a fraud. But the committee wasn't ready to say that, and the public battle of Houdini vs. Margery was well under way in the newspapers.

The public thought that if the committee would not declare Margery a fraud, then she must be a real medium, able to communicate with the world beyond death.

The country was absorbed by the controversy. Hundreds of newspaper stories and editorials were written. For months, letters to the editor were filled with charges and countercharges. Sir Arthur Conan Doyle chimed in with long defenses of Margery's powers, even though he was in England and had never seen her at work. The "Margery Trial" was as widely followed in 1924 as the O. J. Simpson trial and the impeachment trial of President William Jefferson Clinton were in modern times: Everybody had an opinion, everybody wanted a resolution.

The *Scientific American* committee's report didn't satisfy Houdini. The committee voted four to one against her, but it would not say whether Margery was genuine or fake. Houdini shouldered the cause alone. He rented Boston's Symphony Hall for two nights and offered Margery ten thousand dollars to perform her "effects" onstage. Margery declined the challenge. And even though Houdini and Margery never met again, their battle continued.

Houdini intensified his attacks on mediums. He gave more anti- Spiritualist lectures than ever, using the Margery box to show her up publicly. He hired a small group of "psychic investigators" to travel ahead of his tour. They visited prominent mediums and got information that helped him expose their deceit. In 1925, Houdini did undercover investigations himself and went on police raids. He even

Houdini demonstrates the art of making "spirit hands." Mediums used the hands in a number of ways to defraud people attending séances.

testified before a Congressional hearing looking into Spiritualist fraud.

When Houdini publicly exposed fraudulent mediums in a packed theater, there was high drama and anger.

"Christ was persecuted," objected one Spiritualist minister during a Houdini lecture, "and now we Spiritualists are being persecuted. Some day, as in the case of Christ, we will be recognized."

"But Christ never robbed people of two dollars, did he?" Houdini asked, referring to the standard price for communicating with the afterworld.

"Your tricks are frauds," the minister responded. "You are duping the public exactly as you claim Spiritualists are."

"I studied years to do what I am doing. The public knows that I am deceiving them. I give them optical illusions for entertainment, part of which is derived from their efforts to discover how I do it."

Houdini couldn't have said it any better, and he received high praise for his war against fraud from newspapers and magazines. A famous literary critic, Edmund Wilson, wrote that Houdini "appeared to the public in something like his true character and at something like his full stature.... He seemed to take more pleasure in explaining how tricks were done than in astonishing people with them."

Eventually, the power of mediums declined. Houdini had played a major role in unlocking the chains of superstition that shackled millions of honest, grief-stricken people.

Houdini encouraged young people to attend his anti-Spiritualist lectures, hoping that they could grow up free from superstition.

The Master Magician on Broadway

During the winter of 1925-26, all the threads of Houdini's interests and all the desires for his career came together in yet another stunning success. Houdini opened at the 44th Street Theater on Broadway. It was a full evening of *Houdini*, subtitled *Three Shows in One*.

Act one featured magic: Aladdin's Lamp, The Magical Rose Bush, The Flying Handkerchief, and many other illusions. It was the first successful full-scale magic show of his career.

Act two featured Houdini's most evergreen escapes: Metamorphosis and the Chinese Water-Torture Cell.

Act three was titled *"Do the Dead Come Back?"* It was an hour of trickery exposed.

Houdini was the biggest program Houdini had ever presented, with more props and assistants than ever before. Bess Houdini performed along with her niece and cousin. The program was enormously gratifying to the fifty-two-year-old Houdini: "The most successful (financially and artistically) one that I have had."

Not all the reviewers were as enthusiastic as Houdini, but his full-evening show was unquestionably a triumph in theatergoers' eyes.

More than ever before, Houdini thought about retirement. But he was brimming with new enthusiasms and plans for new projects. He was researching an encyclopedia of superstition, drawing up a program of study for a University of Magic he wanted to open, and planning to take English

Chestnut St. Opera House

Week Beginning Monday, February 15, 1926
Matinees Wednesday and Saturday

L. LAWRENCE WEBER

Has the Honor to Offer
MASTER MYSTIFIER

HOUDINI

Acclaimed by Press and Public
"The Greatest Necromancer of the Age—Perhaps of All Times."
(Literary Digest)

Who Presents
AN ENTIRE EVENING'S ENTERTAINMENT
Consisting of Many Original Mysteries Never
Before Equaled in the Realm of Magic Art

"THREE SHOWS IN ONE"
Magic—Illusions—Escapes—and Fraud Mediums Exposed

NOTE—During Houdini's performance it will be necessary to invite a committee of investigators on the stage, and the management assures all volunteers that no practical jokes of any kind will be perpetrated on anyone.
Almost every experiment presented by Houdini is his original invention and creation.

PROGRAM SUBJECT TO CHANGE
In the event that challenges are made and accepted, certain features of the program will be deleted to make space for those added.

SPECIAL MUSICAL SCORE COMPOSED AND ARRANGED BY ORVILLE MAYHOOD

PROGRAM
ACT I
MAGIC

The Crystal Casket
Conradi's Aladdin's Lamp
The Magical Rose Bush
Queen Bess' Bunny
The Arrival and Departure of Ponzi
Izaak Walton Eclipsed
The Mystical Huntsman
The Flying Handkerchief
Intelligent Fingers
Red Magic
Fleurette's Transition

DR. LYNN
Mysterious Effects that Startled and Pleased Your Grand and Great-Grand-Parents
PALIGENESIA
Or Taking a Living Man to Pieces and Restoring Him by Installment
This is an invention of the celebrated Dr. Lynn and was performed by him all over the civilized world and upward of 5,000 times in London, England. Houdini takes pleasure in presenting this mystery, being the only living performer legally authorized to do so, having obtained it from the son of Dr. Lynn, with full permission to present it in public as a matter of historical record for magicians. THE APPARATUS USED IS THE IDENTICAL ORIGINAL, BUILT AND USED BY DR. LYNN.

The Egyptian Turban.
The East Indian Needle Trick.
Metamorphosis—The Exchange of Human Beings in a Locked, Sealed and Corded Trunk.
The Celebrated East Indian Needle Mystery.
Money for Nothing.
Summertime.
Radio of 1950.

Card Sleights—Houdini was the first to present the forward and back palm.
Houdini presents today card manipulations, such as his thirty-two card forward and back palm, which gained for him the title of "King of Cards" more than thirty years ago. Many of his original passes and sleights have been used by most all of the present-day magicians.
The Card Star (Herr Doebler's Masterpiece).
The Miracles of Mahatma.
The Whirlwind of Colors.

Ten Minute Intermission.

ACT II
THE RIBBON CURTAIN
Special attention is called to the blue curtain, which may appear like a crazy-quilt pattern. Twenty-five years ago Houdini, touring Continental Europe, broke records in every theatre in which he appeared. It was the custom in those days to present the artist with a huge laurel wreath, a la Marathon winner, and the ribbons are from the following managers and theatre owners: Berlin Winter Garden, Berlin, Germany; Herr Director Kauszetzer, Central Theatre, Dresden, Saxony; Director Bruck, Frankford a Maine; Director Tichy, Prague, Bohemia; Director Tom Barresford, Alhambra Theatre, Paris, France; Director C. Dundas Slater, Alhambra Theatre, London, England; Director Hippodrome, London, England; Director Harry Rickards, Australia; Director Gluck, Dusseldorf; Director L. Lerin, Rembrandt Theatre, Amsterdam, Holland; Director Corty, Althoff; Director Busch, Berlin; Director Carre, Holland; Director M. Wolf, Essen,

A Philadelphia theater's program for Houdini. *Judging by the number of entries, it was truly a full evening's entertainment.*

classes at Columbia University the next fall. Only Houdini could see himself as both a university dean and a college freshman at the same time.

The summer of 1926 brought an unexpected challenge that Houdini couldn't refuse. Appalled that an amateurish Egyptian magician claimed to be able to go into a trance and survive underwater without air, Houdini plunged in. In August, Houdini was sealed in a bronze casket and held underwater for one and a half hours without air. Once again, Houdini had smashed popular scientific notions. The casket contained only enough air, scientists said, for a man to live three or four minutes. Houdini had proved that men trapped in collapsed mines and similar life-threatening situations could survive by relaxing, breathing slowly, and controlling their fear.

Houdini spent one and a half hours underwater in this airtight coffin to prove that fear, not lack of air, killed miners trapped in airless spaces. Before the experiment, a U. S. government doctor said that the locked coffin held only enough air for three to four minutes of breathing.

Houdini went on tour in September 1926 and almost immediately suffered setbacks. Bess came down with food poisoning in Rhode Island. In Albany, New York, Houdini's ankle was fractured while performing the Chinese Water-Torture Cell. Rather than going to a hospital, he finished the show. A local newspaper called it another example of the master showman's "grit."

Days later, using a splint he had made himself, Houdini performed in Montreal, Canada, and even did a lecture on Spiritualism at McGill University. After the lecture, a student showed Houdini sketches he had drawn of him; Houdini invited the student back to his dressing room for more sketching.

Houdini reclined on a couch to nurse his broken ankle as the artist sketched him and a friend of the artist watched. A third student came unexpectedly and distracted Houdini with questions about miracles of the Bible. He suddenly switched subjects, asking if it was true that Houdini could withstand body punches without being injured. There is no record that Houdini ever made such a claim; reluctantly, he agreed that he could take the punches and allowed the third student to hit him.

Standing tensely over the prone Houdini, the student punched him viciously in the abdomen, twice. The artist and his friend protested, but the third student landed three more powerful blows before Houdini raised his arm and mumbled, "That will do."

As the session ended minutes later, Houdini apologized to the artist for being a poor subject. "The truth is, I don't feel so well," he said. The real truth was much more serious than that.

On the way to Detroit, Bess, still quite sick herself, realized that Houdini was in great pain. She insisted that he see a doctor. The doctor said he needed immediate hospitalization, but Houdini performed before checking in.

Doctors removed Houdini's burst appendix and discovered that the rupture had produced peritonitis. An inflammation of the membrane lining the stomach and intestines, peritonitis usually caused death in less than a day. Houdini hung on for a week, but finally died on Halloween, 1926. He was fifty-two years old. Hardeen, his magician brother, said Houdini's last words were: "Dash, I'm getting tired and I can't fight it any more."

Days earlier, the entire Houdini show had been shipped back to New York except for the bronze coffin Houdini had used for his underwater test in August. As his body was returned to New York in that coffin, lengthy obituaries of Houdini ran in hundreds of newspapers. The next week, theatergoers saw newsreels of the Houdini funeral—a procession of more than fifty cars winding through Manhattan to the Weiss family burial plot in the borough of Queens. Houdini was buried next to his mother with her letters under his head.

HARDEEN
Inherits his Brother's Secrets

"FOURTH: I give, devise and bequeath to my brother, THEODORE, Professionally known as "HARDEEN" .... all my theatrical effects, new mysteries and illusions and accompanying paraphernalia, to be burnt and destroyed upon his death."

Houdini

HOUDINI'S WILL
Makes possible the continuance of
HOUDINI'S MASTER MYSTERIES

Houdini's will left most of his book collection to the Library of Congress. His theatrical collection was left to Bess, and all his stage equipment and performing secrets went to his brother Hardeen. But lacking Houdini's awesome personality, Hardeen's act was never as successful as the original.

The Secret Himself

"The public is a thick-skinned beast and you have to keep whacking it on its hide to let it know you're there."

Walt Whitman, America's greatest poet, said that before Ehrich Weiss was born. Whitman wrote articles about himself, reviewed his own writing anonymously, planted newspaper stories about himself, and even designed his own tomb—all things Houdini did as well. It's unlikely that Houdini knew about Whitman's advice, but he understood it.

Houdini's relentless self-promotion helped make him a star and keep him in the public mind many years after his death. But nobody would remember Houdini if he had not been filled with enthusiasm and curiosity and energy. It was the drive to succeed on his own terms that made him famous. It was devotion to work, to invention, to constant self-improvement that kept him on top. Houdini really was larger than life because he never did anything halfway.

He left his entire act to Hardeen in his will, and Hardeen performed it for years after Houdini's death. But the magic was gone. Houdini was right when he said, "I want my show to be the best of its kind whilst I am alive. When I am dead there will never be another like it."

No magician since Houdini has achieved the fame he had. By 1926, when Houdini died, vaudeville was dying, too. Movies, radio, and television changed people's tastes in entertainment. It's hard to imagine Houdini keeping an audience spellbound for an entire hour today as he struggled behind a curtain. But almost nobody alive today ever saw Houdini hold an audience in the palm of his hand. So who knows?

The secrets? Who knew Houdini's tricks? People searched for years—the Houdini gravesite has often been vandalized by people looking for secrets. Why do they bother? Houdini himself revealed many secrets while he was alive. Famous magicians say that anyone who looks closely at the Milk Can and the Chinese Water-Torture Cell can discover their secrets. But not all magicians agree that we know everything about Houdini. Teller, of the Penn and Teller magic team, claimed, "Finally, although many of Houdini's secrets are known... many others are sealed in death."

Bess Houdini knew him better than anybody else on earth. She had traveled the road with him from circuses and Dime Museums to vaudeville stardom and international fame. She had watched Houdini become a legend and knew that: "He buries no secrets. Every conjuror knows how his tricks were done—with the exception of just where or how the various traps or mechanism were hidden.... It was Houdini himself that was the secret."

Harry Houdini

April 6, 1874—October 31, (Hallowe'en) 1926

"Eyes of Memory Never Sleep"

Bess published this memorial ten years after Houdini's death.

Author's Note

In 1976, biographers Bert Randolph Sugar and the Amazing Randi acknowledged that "the life of Houdini resembles a crazy jigsaw puzzle put together by a drunken carpenter." The core of magic, after all, is misdirection of the audience's attention. Houdini's misdirection never stopped at the footlights.

Through his life, Houdini manipulated the facts to suit his momentary purpose. In the 1890s, Houdini claimed European birth because it added the foreign flavor he thought a magician needed. When public opinion was hostile to Germany and Austria during World War I, he shifted his birthplace to Appleton, Wisconsin.

Determining the facts is further complicated by Houdini's masterful understanding of publicity. Knowing that reporters wanted news, he obligingly fabricated it. As a result, many Houdini stories—his father's duel, Houdini's being shot in the Wild West, or being trapped below the icy Detroit River-that have no factual basis have been repeated by biographers for more than seventy years.

In striving to present the most factual life of Houdini possible, I found the research painstakingly unearthed by Professor Kenneth Silverman of New York University most helpful. Based on more than a decade-long review of original sources (including passenger manifests, police records, and court documents), Silverman's *Houdini!!!* definitively deflates much of the myth Houdini himself invented. It presents a profoundly complex, inventive, and thoughtful man with a genuinely big heart.

Of course, some stories can never be confirmed. Did Houdini's father really make him swear to take care of

Cecilia? Houdini said he did and lived accordingly. In that light, I regard the story as true.

Finally, a very long book could be written about the mechanics of Houdini's escapes; that book would consist mostly of conjecture. There are at least a dozen plausible explanations, for example, of the means he used to open the *London Illustrated Mirror* handcuffs. But nearly a century after the event, Houdini remains the Master of Mystification because nobody knows for sure how it was done.

Chronology

1870 — *Memoirs of Eugene Robert-Houdin* published in English.

March 24, 1874 — Ehrich Weiss (Houdini) born in what is now Budapest, Hungary.

1876 — Mayer Weiss, Ehrich's father, came to the U.S. by himself looking for work; the telephone was invented by Alexander Graham Bell, a Scottish immigrant.

1878 — Ehrich traveled to U.S. with his mother and siblings; the Weiss family settled in Appleton, WI.

1883 (?) — "Ehrich, the Prince of Air" performed in a Milwaukee, WI back yard.

1886 — Ehrich, aged 12, ran away to Texas looking for work.

1887 — The Weiss family moved to New York City; Arthur Conan-Doyle published the first Sherlock Holmes story in London.

1891 (?) — Ehrich Weiss took the stage name Harry Houdini.

October 5, 1892 — Rabbi Mayer Weiss, Houdini's father, died of cancer; Thomas Alva Edison patented the motion picture camera.

June 22, 1894 — Wilhelmina Beatrice Rahner and Houdini marry; the Houdinis principal stage feat is Metamorphosis.

1895-98 — The Houdinis performed without much success in a number of circuses and theatrical troupes touring the U.S. and Canada.

1899 — The Houdinis broke into vaudeville under Martin Beck's management; aspirin was invented.

1900 — Houdini introduced the Nude Jail Cell Escape in April; he debuted in Europe as "The King of Handcuffs" in July.

1903 — The Wright Brothers fly the first heavier-than-air machine, or airplane.

1904 — Houdini needed more than one-and-a-half hours to escape the *London Illustrated Mirror* handcuffs.

1905 — Houdini and Bess buy a New York brownstone at 278 West 113th St.

1908 — Introduced the Milk Can Escape and published *The Unmasking of Robert-Houdin*; Ford introduced the Model T, the first mass-produced, widely affordable car.

1910 — Houdini made first successful airplane flight on the Australian continent.

1912 — Houdini introduced Chinese Water-Torture Cell; the *Titanic* hit an iceberg and sank.

July 17, 1913 — Cecelia Weiss, Houdini's mother, died.

1914 — Houdini met former-President Theodore Roosevelt returning to the U. S. in May; By year's end, World War I involved thirty-two countries.

1915 — Suspended Straitjacket Escape introduced.

1917 — After United States entered WWI, Houdini made dozens of benefit appearances.

1918 — An armistice, or short truce, on 11 November finally ends World War I; influenza pandemic kills over 20 million people.

1919 — *The Master Mystery*, Houdini's first film, was successful world-wide.

1920 — Houdini and Sir Arthur Conan-Doyle became friends; KDKA in Pittsburgh became the first commercial radio station.

1921 — Houdini published *Miracle Mongers and Their Methods.*

1923 — *Haldane of the Secret Service,* Houdini's fifth and final film, opened in theaters.

1924 — *A Magician Among the Spirits* published; Houdini toured the U.S. lecturing against fraudulent mediums.

1926 — Houdini's biggest show opened on Broadway; on 31 October, he died from peritonitis following an appendectomy.

1927 — *The Jazz Singer* opened, the first movie with a recorded sound track; Charles Lindbergh made the first solo trans-Atlantic flight.

Bibliography

Spellbinder

Blumenthal, Sidney. *Coming to America*. New York: Delacorte Press, 1981

Boorstin, Daniel J. et al, *We Americans*. Washington, DC: National Geographic Society, 1975

Brandon, Ruth. *The Life and Many Deaths of Harry Houdini*. New York: Random House, 1994,

Brownlow, Kevin. *The Parade's Gone By*. New York: Alfred A. Knopf, 1968

Cannell, J. C. *The Secrets of Houdini*. New York: Dover Publications, 1973

Christopher, Milbourne *Houdini: the Untold Story*. New York: Pocket Books, 1975

———*Houdini: A Pictorial Biography*. New York: Grammercy, 1998

———*The Illustrated History of Magic*. New York: Crowell, 1973

Faulkner, Harold V. *Politics, Reform and Expansion: 1890-1900*. New York: Harper & Brothers, 1959

Fitzsimons, Raymund. *Death and the Magician: The Mystery of Houdini*. New York: Atheneum ,1981

Gibson, Walter B. & Young, Morris N. *Houdini on Magic*. New York: Dover Publications, Inc., 1953

Henning, Doug with Reynolds, Charles. *Houdini: His Legend And His Magic.* New York: Times Books, 1977

Houdini, Harry. *Miracle Mongers and Their Methods: A Complete Expose.* Buffalo, NY: Prometheus Books, 1993

———*The Unmasking of Robert-Houdin.* New York: The Publishers Printing Co. 1908

Johnson, Paul. *A History of the American People.* New York: Harper Collins Publishers, 1997

Kellock ,Harold. *Houdini: His Life-Story.* New York: Blue Ribbon Books, 1931

Kennedy, David M. *Over Here: The First World War and American Society.* New York: Oxford University Press, 1980

Meyer, Bernard C. *Houdini: A Mind In Chains: A Psychoanalytic Portrait.* New York: Dutton, 1976

Randi, Amazing & Sugar, Bert Randolph. *Houdini: His Life And Art.* New York: Grosset & Dunlap, 1976

White, Florence. *Escape!: The Life of Harry Houdini.* New York : J. Messner, 1979

About the Author

Enjoyed equally by adults and kids, *Houdini: The Ultimate Spellbinder* plunged Tom Lalicki so deeply into Houdiniana that he followed up the award-winning biography with three Houdini & Nate crime novels. They are *Danger in the Dark*, *Shots at Seas*, and *Frame-Up on the Bowery*, also available as ebooks.

A real-life Bruce Wayne, Houdini was the first American superhero. The world's greatest entertainer was a secretive philanthropist who used his nearly supernatural physical and mental powers to unmask villainy and capture criminals.

OPEN **(I)** ROAD

INTEGRATED MEDIA

Open Road Integrated Media is a digital publisher
and multimedia content company. Open Road
creates connections between authors and their
audiences by marketing its ebooks through a new
proprietary online platform, which uses premium
video content and social media.

www.ingramcontent.com/pod-product-compliance
Lightning Source LLC
Chambersburg PA
CBHW051847040426
42447CB00006B/735